MW00380211

This book is dedicated to chinchillas and their devoted parents everywhere.

CHAPTER 1

Introduction
to Chinchillas

Chinchillas are smart, curious, and energetic animals. Their sweet personalities and lively spirits make them a joy to keep as pets. However, they are not a suitable pet for everyone. This book will cover everything from feeding and housing your chinchilla to common health issues.

The first thing you need to know about chinchillas is that they have a long lifespan of up to 15-20 years. This makes them a huge commitment. Be prepared to have your furry friend around for many, many years. If you aren't prepared to spend the next 20 years taking care of your chinchillas, they aren't the right fit for you and your family.

Chinchillas are also highly social animals. They should be kept in same sex pairs so they don't get lonely. They enjoy cuddling and snuggling with each other, and having a companion can really help increase their quality of life. Make sure to properly sex them before putting them together to ensure there are no unexpected pregnancies. Introducing chinchillas to each other can be tricky. We'll discuss introductions in detail in a later chapter.

They have a large range of noises that they make in order to communicate to one another. The most common noises are the bark, kack, and peep. The bark is a loud squeak that signals when the chinchilla is scared or upset. The kack is a sharp, quick sort of squeak that is usually a warning signal that your chinchilla is irrated or angry. When a chinchilla is happy or curious, it will make very soft peeping noises.

One important fact you need to know about chinchillas is that they are crepuscular. Crepuscular animals are most active at dawn and dusk. They should be kept in a low traffic area of the house so they can sleep soundly during the daytime. Unlike nocturnal pets, they will wake up every now and then during the day to eat, drink, or play. Most don't mind being woken up for playtime or socialization throughout the day, but they prefer to do most of their activities in the early mornings and early evenings.

Another highly important fact about chinchillas is that they have extremely soft, dense fur. They have 80 hairs per follicle. Humans only have 1-3 hairs per follicle, so you can imagine how thick a chin's fur is. Having such dense fur means that you should never bathe a chinchilla in water or get them wet. Due to its density, the fur takes an incredibly long time to dry. When the hair is wet for long periods of time, it can cause a fungal infection on the skin. It can also cause the chinchilla to become very cold, and the chinchilla could run the risk of getting pneumonia. So, how do you bathe a chinchilla if you can't get them wet? With dust! I know what you're

Chinchillas are most active at dawn and dusk.

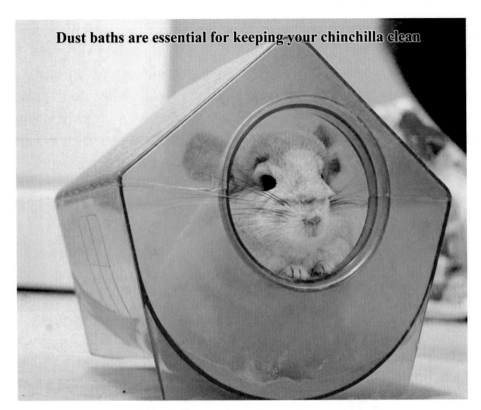
Dust baths are essential for keeping your chinchilla clean

probably thinking. How does dust get a chinchilla clean? In the wild, chinchillas live in a dry, arid climate. To stay clean, they regularly roll in volcanic ash. This strips the oils and moisture from the fur and leaves it fluffy and clean.

Giving your chinchilla a dust bath is super easy. You should always use a dust specifically made to be used for chinchillas. Dusting is a natural behavior, and your chinchilla will instinctively roll in the dust immediately. The best way to dust your chinchilla is to place the dust in a bath house or other container that the chinchilla can easily get in and out of and have room to roll in. A bath house with a closed top is preferable since it will keep most of the dust from getting all over the floor. Your chinchilla does not need a dust bath every day. 3-4 times per week is preferable, and you should only leave the bath house in the cage for 10 minutes each time. Dusting too frequently can dry out your chinchilla's skin. Leaving the dust in the cage too long can result in your chinchilla urinating in the dust. If they roll around in the soiled dust, it can cause eye infections or irritation.

A Brief History

Chinchillas originate from the Andes Mountains in South America. Their habitat is cold and dry with little vegetation They have many natural enemies like snakes and birds. To escape these enemies, they burrow and hide in rock crevices. They live in large social groups to help protect them from predators.

Chinchillas originate from the cold, arid Andes Mountains.

In the 1600s, Spanish conquistadores discovered the chinchilla and quickly realized their potential in the fur industry. In the 1900s, demand for their fur from Europe and America drove them to the brink of extinction. In 1923, Mathias F. Chapman traveled to South America to attempt to bring chinchillas to the United States. No one had ever been able to successfully trap chinchillas and get them safely from the mountains to the ground without overheating. Chapman slowly brought them down the mountain so they could acclimate to the warmer temperatures. He successfully brought down eleven chinchillas. He shipped them to California and kept them cool with ice packed around them. One female gave birth on the trip. Although he originally brought them to the US for use in the fur industry, all pet chinchillas today come from Chapman's original eleven.

In general, Chinchillas are energetic, inquisitive, smart, and playful. They love to explore their surroundings. Each chinchilla has a unique personality. Some chinchillas are shy. Some are outgoing. Most hate being held while others don't mind being picked up every now and then. If you're looking for a super cuddly pet, chinchillas might not be a good fit for you.

They can easily jump up to 3-6 feet high. They are extremely agile and can squeeze into very tiny spaces. Chinchillas also love "wall surfing", meaning they literally bounce off the walls. They can also sprint around a room at top speed. This can make them very hard to catch. If a chinchilla is grabbed and they get scared, they fur slip. This means that they will shed the fur where they are being grabbed. In the wild, they use this as a defense mechanism to escape predators. Don't be alarmed if this happens to your chinchilla. The hair will grow back.

Chinchillas rarely bite. A few

Always hold your chinchilla properly to avoid injury.

reasons a chinchilla might bite are stress, fear, or illness. Chinchillas who haven't been socialized with humans are more likely to bite than those with daily human interaction. Chinchilla bites can be very painful, however, it's important not to show anger or punish your chinchilla for biting. This would only cause more stress and fear for the chinchilla.

Another way chinchillas

express fear and stress is urine spraying. They will stand up and spray a stream of urine. Chinchillas also occasionally spray each other when fighting for dominance. While it's more common for females, males also have the ability to urine spray.

To pick up your chinchilla, don't grab them by their midsection. This can injure them. Try scooping them up with your hand slid underneath them and grab the very base of their tail with your other hand. If your chinchilla runs away and won't let you pick it up, do not chase your chinchilla around to try to catch it. This can be very stressful.

Along with other rodents like guinea pigs, mice, and rats, when chinchillas are happy they "popcorn". Popcorning is a hop straight up in the air. When some people first witness this behavior, they become concerned something is wrong with their chinchilla, but don't worry. It's normal, and it's pretty cute!

The more you socialize with your chinchilla, the friendlier he or she will be. It's important not to try to do too much with a new chinchilla too fast. Start by talking softly to them for a few days. You can even read a book to them if you can't find

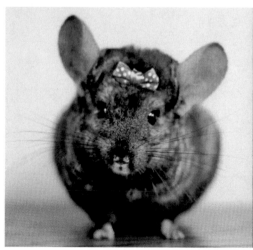

Daily socialization will lead to a friendlier chinchilla

Popcorning is a sign of happiness

anything to talk about. They will get used to your voice and learn to trust you. Once you've earned their trust by talking to them, put your hand in the cage and let them come to you. You can put a treat in your hand, and try to get them to come up to you and take the treat. If you do this long enough, eventually your chinchilla may even walk right into your hand. Once you feel comfortable with the bond you've established with your chinchilla, you can allow them to run free in a chinchilla proofed room. Bathrooms often work well for this because they have very few surfaces for them to chew on or holes for them to squeeze into. Once your chinchilla is out of the cage, it can be tricky to catch them. If you are having difficulty catching your chinchilla, wait until he or she goes inside their dust bath house and cover the opening with a book or other object. Do not try using your hand because your chinchilla could get scared and bite. Once they are safely in the bath house, you can carry it all the way back to their cage and place it inside.

CHAPTER 2

Housing your
Chinchilla

Choosing a suitable cage is important for the health and happiness of your chinchilla

Cages

When choosing the best cage for your chinchilla, there are a few things to consider. The first thing you should look at is bar spacing. If you have a very young chinchilla, 8-12 weeks, you will want to find 1/2 inch spacing or less so your chinchilla doesn't escape through the bars. For adult chins, spacing up to one inch wide is acceptable.

The next thing you need to look for in a cage is the size. The minimum cage size for adult chinchillas is 3 feet wide by 2 feet tall and 2 feet deep. Personally, I find that tall, multi-level cages

work best. Chinchillas need a lot of vertical space to jump around, so a shorter cage made for guinea pigs or rabbits is not suitable. Tanks and aquariums are also not a suitable choice. They don't allow enough ventilation, and they can get very warm which can overheat a chinchilla very easily. The lack of ventilation causes ammonia from the urine to build up, and this can cause respiratory infections. A cage with bars is always the best choice.

Another thing to avoid when picking out a cage is a wire floor.

These wire mesh floors can be very hard on chinchilla feet. Standing on the wire can cause a condition known as bumblefoot. Bumblefoot, or plantar pododermatitis, is an inflammatory reaction caused by a bacterial infection. One more reason to avoid wire floors in your cage is that your chinchilla's feet and legs can fall through the holes. If your chinchilla's leg slips through and they try to jump, they can easily injure or break their leg. Your chinchilla's cage should not have any plastic in it. If you do have a cage with plastic shelves, you should remove them and replace them with wood shelves. You will also want a cage with a strong latch so your chinchilla can not escape.

Pictured above is a great example of a very safe three story cage with plenty of wood shelves, things to climb on, and more than enough space.

If your cage is four feet tall or taller, you will want to make sure you have a shelf or hammock going across the width of your cage to catch your chinchilla if he/she happens to fall from a top shelf. Some cages come with ramps leading up to the shelves. Since chinchillas can jump long distances, they do not need these ramps.

It's important to know that if you already have a large cage, you may be able to fix it up to be perfect for your chinchilla.

Pictured below on the left is a used cage with a few unsafe elements. On the right, you will see the updated cage. Notice the hammock going across the middle to catch any falling chinchillas. Also, note that the wire shelves and ramps have been removed and replaced with wood. If you have a cage with wire or plastic shelves, you can easily remove them and replace them with wood yourself.

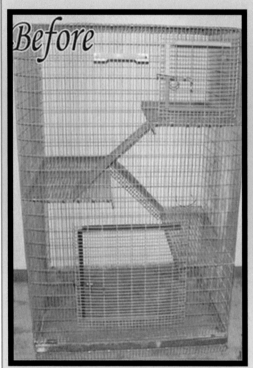

Shelves

Shelves are important for every chinchilla cage. They should be made from kiln dried pine wood. You can find this wood at most hardware stores. Do not use other types of wood like cedar or birch. To make your own shelves, you can cut the wood to any size you need. If you don't have a saw, some hardware stores will cut the wood for you. After cutting, you need to sand all edges so they are smooth. To attach the shelves to the cage,

you will have to add hanger bolts, wing nuts, and washers. To attach the hanger bolts, first drill a hole in the back of the shelf. Use a drill bit that is slightly smaller than your hanger bolts. Next, screw the wing nut onto the hanger bolt. You can attach the hanger bolt to the shelf by using the wing nut to screw the hanger bolt into the wood. When you are finished, it should look like the upper right image.

Wheels

It is important to choose a safe wheel for your chinchilla. Many wheels are made of a wire mesh. These wheels are extremely unsafe. Chinchillas' feet can easily fall through the holes, and if a leg or foot falls through while running, the leg can easily break. There have been many cases of chinchillas needing leg amputations after breaking their leg on a wire wheel. Another unsafe option is plastic. Chinchillas will chew anything they can get their teeth on, including a plastic wheel.

Plastic wheels are not safe for chinchillas

A safe wheel needs to be 15" in diameter or larger. It should also be made of solid metal so your chinchilla can not chew it. There are two options available. One is a normal round upright wheel. The next safe option is a saucer or disc wheel. These wheels are great because chinchillas don't have to arch their back to use them.

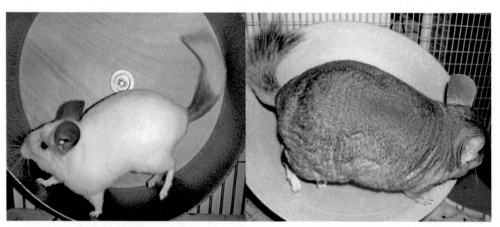

This chinchilla is using a safe 15" metal and wood wheel.

This chinchilla is using a safe flying saucer or disc wheel

BEDDING OPTIONS

You will need to select a safe bedding material for your chinchilla's cage. There are many options available, but which one should you choose?

ASPEN	If you're looking for the best wood shavings, aspen is the number one choice. It is 100% safe.
PINE	Pine shavings are also a good choice, but make sure it's kiln dried pine. If it's not kiln dried, it's not safe.
CAREFRESH (Wood pulp and cellulose)	This bedding comes in many colors from brown and white to pink, purple, and yellow. It is very absorbent and controls odor well. If you choose this bedding, you have to monitor your chinchilla carefully and make sure he or she isn't chewing or eating any of it. If ingested, it does not digest well and can cause intestinal problems.
NEWSPAPER	There are many better options than newspaper as bedding. It isn't absorbent and can lead to stained fur from sitting on the soiled papers. However, newspaper is great to put under whatever bedding you decide to use.
SAWDUST	Chinchillas have sensitive respiratory systems. Since sawdust is so fine, they can breathe it in, and it can irritate their respiratory system or even cause a respiratory infection.
CEDAR	Cedar bedding is toxic! It contains volatile phenols that are released into the air. Studies show that animals housed on cedar bedding have drastic changes in their liver enzymes and a high risk of asthma or respiratory infections which can be fatal.

Fleece as Bedding

You're probably thinking fleece fabric is for blankets not for animal bedding, but if done correctly, fleece is the best bedding available by far! It's comfortable, easy to do, and the best part is that it's washable! You can reuse your fleece liners over and over again which makes them one of the cheapest bedding options you can find.

How do you use fleece as bedding? There are a few different ways. Many chinchilla supply sellers have an array of fleece liners for sale. You can also easily make your own fleece liners. All you need is a yard of either anti-pill or blizzard fleece per liner, a sewing machine, thread, and an absorbent material. This absorbent material will go under a layer of fleece. You can use a towel, quilt batting, or another layer of fleece. Before you start to sew your liner, you need to wash and dry the fleece fabric twice. Do not use fabric softener when washing the fleece. Measure the size you need to cover with the fleece, and add 1.5 inches to each side then cut your fleece and absorbent layer to the appropriate sizes. You will need two same sized pieces of fleece, one for the top layer and one for the bottom layer.

Place your absorbent layer on the bottom then layer your bottom fleece design face up on top of the absorbent layer. Next, place your top layer with the design facing down on top of the previous layer. You need to place them this way so the liner ends up with the design on the outside after you flip it inside out. Once you have them set up in the right order, you can pin the layers together to make them easier to sew. Now you're ready to start sewing.

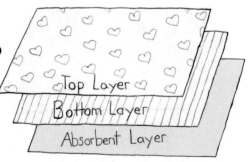

Top Layer
Bottom Layer
Absorbent Layer

Depending on your cage setup, you can choose to do a liner that sits at the bottom of the cage (figure 1) or if your cage has a shelf or pan that you want to line, you can make a pillow case style liner (figure 2). This style of liner is completely open at one end so you can slip it over the shelf or pan with ease. Simply sew three sides as pictured. Flip the liner inside out, and you're ready to use your new liner. It is important to have your top layer be at least 6" longer than the size of your pan or shelf. This is so you can tuck the excess fabric under the pan so the liner is closed on all sides once in the cage. For the closed liner (figure 1), you will need to sew all four sides leaving a small gap on one of the sides so you can flip the liner inside out. Once flipped, you can sew the gap that you left open.

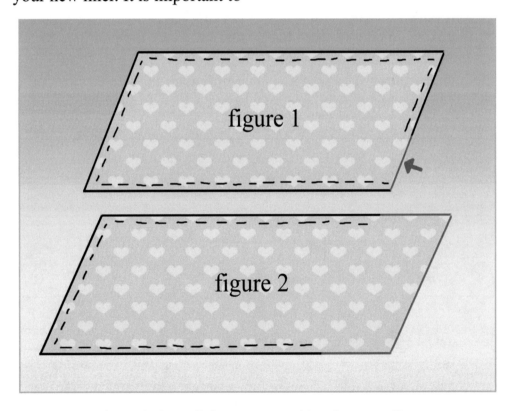

Figure 1: Sew all the way around leaving a small gap
Figure 2: Sew three sides and leave one end open

To wash your fleece, you need to remove it from the cage and shake all of the hay, food, and poops off. Once it's clean, put the liner in your washing machine. Only use detergent to clean your liners. Never use fabric softener. You can also pour some vinegar in with your liner to help reduce odor. The liner can either be air dried or put in the dryer with no dryer sheets.

Fleece does require some daily upkeep. You will need to vacuum or sweep the poops off the liner each day. The liners should be washed a minimum of once per week. You may want to have two sets of liners available so you can use one set while the other is being washed.

You can place a litter pan on top of your fleece liner to encourage your chinchilla to use the liner less. Glass baking dishes work well as a litter pan. Remember to never use plastic. Fill the pan with one of the other safe bedding options mentioned previously. Aspen is a good choice. Place the pan in a corner of the cage. The pan should be emptied and refilled twice per week.

*Fleece is the only safe fabric for liners since it doesn't contain threads that can unravel if chewed and get wrapped around limbs or other body parts causing injury.

Houses

Your chinchilla should have somewhere to hide and sleep in during the day. Being in a dark, enclosed space will make your chinchilla feel secure. Hiding houses should be made of wood, ceramic, or other safe materials and not plastic. It's also important that the house you choose is not made with nails. Chinchillas can chew the edges of the house esposing the nail and making it easy for your chinchilla to get cut when jumping around. If you would like to make your own wood house, you can use a non-toxic wood glue instead of nails to hold the pieces together.

Cage Accessories

Your chinchilla needs a variety of items in their cage to keep them happy and enrich their lives. These are just a few of the many options available.

HAMMOCKS	You can purchase premade hammocks or make your own. They should only be made of fleece.
PUMICE LEDGES	These are wonderful for chinchillas. They give your chinchilla another object to jump and climb on, and they also are safe to chew.
TUBES AND TUNNELS	PVC pipe works well as a tunnel. The PVC must be covered with fleece so it can not be chewed. Large cardboard tubes also work well. Cardboard tubes do not need to be covered with fleece. The diameter of the tube or tunnel should be over 6 inches.
TOYS	There's a large variety of toys available. Toys are a great accessory, but they are also a necessity.

Tube

Hammock

Pumice
Ledge

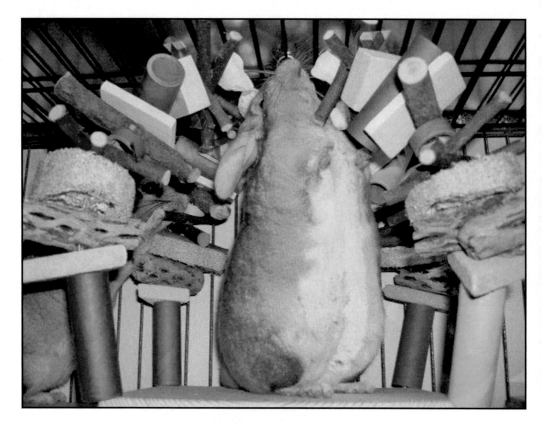

Toys

Toys are necessary to keep your chinchilla occupied, happy, and in good health. Most importantly, these toys help file down their teeth and keep them from getting overgrown. Chinchillas need to chew constantly since their teeth never stop growing.

There is a large variety of safe toys you can purchase or make yourself. Purchasing toys can be tricky since many of the products sold as "safe for chinchillas" are very misleading.

Be creative when making toys for your chinchilla. Mix different materials together, play with shapes, and have fun! Your chinchilla will be happier and healthier from the toys you make.

Safe Toy Parts

WILLOW BALLS	Chinchillas love ripping willow balls apart. They are safe and a great addition to any toy. You can find them in many different sizes and colors.
WOOD BLOCKS	They should be made from a chinchilla safe wood. Wood blocks are usually made of kiln dried pine.
PUMICE STONE	Pumice stone is a porous volcanic rock. Chinchillas really love chewing pumice, and the gritty texture makes it great for their teeth.
BAGEL BITES	Bagel Bites are small cardboard rings that are safe to chew.
WOOD STICKS	Wood chew sticks are one of chinchillas' favorite things. The sticks need to be properly processed and made from a safe wood.
LOOFAH	Loofah is safe to chew after being processed. You can also grow your own loofah.
PALM LEAF	Chinchillas love to shred palm leaf. You can get palm leaf in many shapes and sizes.
BAMBOO SHREDDERS	These are basically just Chinese finger traps, but you need to purchase shredders that are meant for animals. The traps meant for children may be treated with something that might not be safe for chinchillas.
CHOLLA	Cholla is made from a dried cactus plant although it often gets mistaken for a hard wood.

*You can string these toy parts on a wire and hang them in your cage with metal clasps. If you purchase colored toy parts, make sure they were dyed with safe materials such as food coloring or sugar free Kool-Aid.

WOOD STICK

PALM LEAF

LOOFAH

CHOLLA

PUMICE

BAGEL BITE

WILLOW BALL

SAFE TOYS

CHAPTER 3

Food and Treats

Pellets

Choosing the right pellets is very important to the health of your chinchilla. When selecting a pellet, the first thing you want to look for is a pellet with no colorful pieces, no dried fruits, no seeds, and no nuts. The food should contain nothing but plain pellets. Food mixes containing many different colors and seeds are full of fat and sugar.

A safe feed will look like this with plain pellets and nothing else added

The pellet you choose should also have timothy hay or alfalfa hay listed as the first ingredient. You will also want to make sure corn is not listed as an ingredient. Corn is difficult for chinchillas to digest. The pellets should be high in fiber preferably 18-20%. They should be low in fat with around 2-4% maximum and a protein level of of around 15%.

This is a good example of what not to feed your chinchilla

Recommended Brands

Oxbow
Crude Protein min 16.00 %
Crude Fat min 2.50 %
Crude Fiber min 18.00 %
Crude Fiber max 23.00 %

Manna Pro Show Rabbit
Crude Protein Min 16.00 %
Crude Fat Min 3.50 %
Crude Fiber Min 18.00 %
Crude Fiber Max 23.00 %

Mazuri
Crude protein not less than 20.0%
Crude fat not less than 3.0%
Crude fiber not more than 18.0%

Tradition
Crude Protein (min) 17%
Crude Fat (min) 3%
Crude Fiber (max) 16%

Hay

Your chinchilla should be fed an unlimited amount of hay each day. Chinchillas should have access to hay at all times. It is essential for keeping their teeth filed and preventing them from getting overgrown. Timothy hay should be fed daily to adult chinchillas while alfalfa should be fed to young chinchillas and pregnant or nursing chinchillas.

You can occasionally feed other tastier varieties of hay like orchard grass, botanical hay, bluegrass hay, and more. These shouldn't be fed daily, but they can be used every now and then as a treat. You can also feed hay cubes as a treat.

Water

Your chinchilla should have access to fresh water at all times. You will need to clean the water bottle and refill it each day. Using filtered water is recommended since tap water can contain bacteria and parasites like Giardia which can cause diarrhea or constipation. These can be very serious in chinchillas and it can sometimes even be fatal. Make sure the water purifier you purchase states that it eliminates the Giardia parasite.

Chinchillas should always drink from a water bottle and not a water bowl or dish. Since chinchillas should not get wet, water bowls could be a potential hazard.

Treats

Treats you can purchase from a pet store might have a chinchilla on the package, but that does not mean that they are safe. Many pet store treats marketed towards chinchillas are very dangerous. If sugar is one of the first ingredients listed, don't buy the treats. If fruit or nuts are in the treats, you don't want to purchase those either. Treats can be used as a training tool, but they are not an essential part of a chinchilla's diet. Treats should be giving sparingly. Do not feed more than one at a time and no more than 3-4 days a week.

Only feed your chinchilla safe treats and limit all safe treats to only a few days per week.

Safe Treats

ROSEHIPS	Rosehips contain plenty of vitimin C and chinchillas love them. You can feed them whole or crushed. Some chinchillas prefer the crushed because the fibers in the whole rosehips tickle their nose.
SHREDDED WHEAT	Unfrosted shredded wheat is safe to give your chinchilla. You should feed them no more than 1 per day and no more than 3-4 days per week.
ROLLED OATS	Old fashioned rolled oats can be fed as a treat, and chinchillas love them. You can feed a small pinch of oats a few times per week.
GOJI BERRIES	These have a bit of sugar, but less than raisins. You can feed them to your chinchilla, but no more than one a week.
DRIED HIBISCUS FLOWERS	These are also high in vitimin C and they can help prevent constipation.
DRIED ROSEBUDS	These are safe to feed chinchillas and can help improve the skin.
HAY CUBES	Hay cubes are simply compressed hay. You can feed unlimited amounts of timothy hay cubes, but limit alfalfa hay cubes to only one per week.

TREATS TO AVOID

RAISINS	Despite what many websites suggest, raisins are NOT a safe treat. They contain 70% sugar. Too much sugar is unhealthy for chinchillas.
SEEDS AND NUTS	Chinchillas should not be fed any seeds or nuts. They are very high in fat.
PET STORE TREATS	Most treats marketed towards chinchillas can be very dangerous. It's best to avoid all treats sold at pet stores just to be safe.

Fruits and Vegetables

Chinchillas should not be fed fresh fruits or vegetables at any time. They have a very sensitive digestive system and are hindgut fermenters. This means that they have a very hard time processing sugar which most fruit is full of. In the wild, chinchillas eat a very dry diet. The moisture in the fruits and vegetables can cause bloat, diarrhea, or other serious issues. All of the nutrition your chinchilla needs will be provided by the pellets and hay. They simply do not need fruit or vegetables, and it is not worth taking the risk.

Wood

Wood is essential for the health of your chinchilla. But what types of wood should you choose? You can use wood to make shelves and toys, but you can also give your chinchilla processed wood sticks for them to chew on. The wood must be processed properly and made from a safe type of wood.

You can purchase pre-processed wood, but you can also process your own. First, you need to make sure none of the wood you are using came from trees treated with pesticides or other chemicals. Cut the wood to the size you prefer using garden pruners or, if your wood is very thick, you can use a saw. Be extremely careful because this can be very dangerous. Then scrub the wood extremely well to remove lichen, moss, or anything else that may be on the wood. Next, boil the wood to remove any extra dirt that may still be on the wood. Boil the wood for at least 20 minutes. Very carefully strain the water and rinse the wood with cold water. Place the wood on a towel to air dry until the wood no longer looks wet. Preheat the oven to 350 degrees and bake the wood on a baking sheet for 30 minutes. Turn the heat down to 250 degrees and bake for another 30 minutes. If the wood is still not dry, continue baking until it's done. When you can feel the wood is completely dry and you can see small cracks on the inside of the wood, it's time to take it out of the oven. Wait for the wood to cool. Now it is ready for your chinchilla.

Safe Woods

Apple	Chinese Dogwood
Cottonwood	Kiwi
Crab-Apple	Pine (Kiln Dried)
Pear	Alderberry
Mulberry	Grape
Hazelnut	Manzanita
Elm	Hawthorn
Arancariaceae	Magnolia
Roseace	Pecan
Dogwood Rose	Willow

Unsafe Woods

Woods that produce fruits with pits (example: cherry, plum)	Hydrangea	Rosewood
	Eucalptus	Black Locust
	Spruce	Maple
Cashew	Fir	Blackwood
Cedar	Aralia Spinosa	Almond
Cherry	Juniper	Myrtle
All Citrus woods	Green Heart	Mahogany
Elderberry Bushes	Beech	Wenge
Box Elder	Yew	Chinese Snake Tree
Chestnut	Oak	Cypress
Ebony	Teak	Tallow
Sandalwood	Walnut	Lime Tree
Ginko	Ironwood	Sycamore

Chinchilla "Cookie" Recipe

What's more fun than being able to make your chinchillas some delicious, nutritious treats? Chinchillas go crazy for these, and you can make them by following a few easy steps. And what's better is that you can usually make them with ingredients you already have in your home.

To get started, you will need:

*Pellets   *Flour   *Blender, Grinder
*Hay   *Water   or Hammer
*Oats   *Bowl   *Baking Pan

STEP 1

Start by taking one cup of pellets and grinding them into a powder. You can do this by using a blender or grinder, but if you don't have one available, you can put the pellets in a baggie and crush them with a hammer.

STEP 2

At the bottom of most bags of hay is a lot of powdery stuff and hay you can't really feed your chinchilla. Well, now you can!

You will need 1/4 cup of the powdery hay from the bottom of the bag. If you don't have enough fine hay at the bottom of your bag you can grind the hay in a blender or grinder. Add the hay to your crushed pellets.

You can use any type of hay that you would like. If your chinchilla loves orchard grass, you can use that. You can also use alfalfa or timothy hay. It's entirely up to you.

STEP 3

Add 1/4 cup of old fashioned rolled oats. Grind half of the oats and leave the rest of them whole.

STEP 4

Add some water to your mixture. Add a little water at a time to lightly coat the ingredients to the point that they form a paste. You don't want the mixture to be too wet or the cookies won't dry properly.

STEP 5

Add flour a little at a time until the mixture sticks together. You don't want to add too much flour, so check your mixture frequently.

STEP 6

Preheat the oven to 200 degrees. Cover a cookie sheet or pan with aluminum foil. Form the mixture into one inch circles approximately 1/4" thick, and place them on the aluminum foil. Don't make them too thick. Bake them for 20 minutes or until they are dry. Flip the cookies halfway through.

Let the cookies cool, and then they're ready for your chinchilla to taste test! Don't give your chinchilla more than one. Also, limit them to no more than 2-3 per week. You can also experiment with them by adding hibiscus, crushed rosehips, or other safe treats. Store them in a sealed bag to keep them fresh.

CHAPTER
4

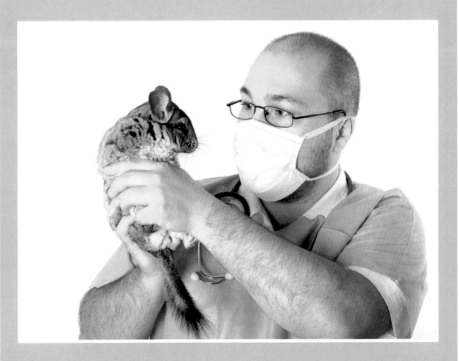

Health and
Safety

Health & Safety Risks

PLASTIC	You should never have any plastic items in your chinchilla's cage. Chinchillas will chew anything and everything. Chewing plastic can cause a blockage in your chinchilla's system that may require surgery or could even be fatal.
EXERCISE BALLS	You can find these large exercise balls at most pet stores, but while they may have a chinchilla on the box, that does not make them safe. Many chinchillas have died in these plastic balls. They don't allow enough ventilation which can cause your chinchilla to overheat and get heat stroke very easily. Do not purchase one of these excercise balls.
LARGE GAPS	Chinchillas can fit their heads into very small spaces, but they can not always get it back out. Be careful of items with large wire spacing: hay balls, hay holders, cage bars, toys, etc. Chinchillas have been known to get their necks broken in some of these items.
ELECTRICAL CORDS	Make sure your chinchilla can not access any electrical cords when they are out of their cage. If they chew on these cords, they run the risk of getting shocked which can cause burns, mouth problems, and even death.
HARNESS	You should never put a harness on your chinchilla. If they pull too hard while wearing a harness, they can easily break their ribs or sustain internal injury.

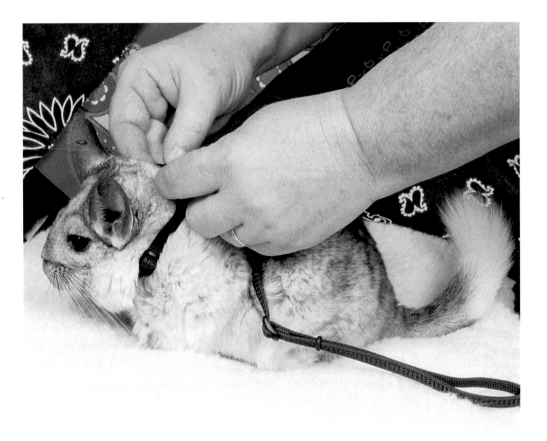

Never put your chinchilla in a harness.

It's just as important to know what's bad for your chinchilla as it is to know what's good for them. Recognizing potential hazards will help you keep your chinchilla safe and healthy.

Exercise balls can cause heat stroke. Chinchillas can also urinate in them, and the urine will get all over their fur when they're running around. Since you can't get chinchillas wet, it's very hard to get the urine stains off their fur.

Veterinary Care

Before acquiring any exotic pet, it is essential to research vets in your area and make sure you have an exotics vet you can easily get to if your pet needs medical attention. Many vets only see cats and dogs, so you will need to call around and make sure the vet you choose will be able to see your chinchilla. If you can not find an exotics vet within a reasonable distance, chinchillas are not the right pet for you.

Along with finding your permanent vet, you will also need to find an emergency vet in your area that sees exotics. If your chinchilla has an accident and needs immediate vet care at any hour of the day or night, they will have to see an emergency vet. It's a good idea to have an emergency vet fund set aside so you can afford to pay for any unforseen vet bills.

"If you can't afford the vet, don't get the pet"

We all run into unfortunate circumstances from time to time. If you need to take your chinchilla to the vet and you aren't able to pay the bill, there are a few options available for you to consider.

CareCredit	You can apply for CareCredit. It works like a credit card, and you can use it to pay your vet bills. Go to www.carecredit.com to apply.
Borrow	It can be hard asking friends and family for money, but sometimes it's the best option available.
Payment Plans	Talk with your vet if you can't afford treatment. Many vets are willing to work with you and some will set up monthly payment plans.

Not taking your pet to the vet is never the right decision. If you can't find a way to get your chinchilla to the vet, the kindest thing you can do is surrender your chinchilla to someone who can.

This book will cover many health concerns, but it is only meant to educate you about these potential issues. It is not meant as a substitute for veterinary care. If your chinchilla has any health problems, you need to see a vet right away. You should never try to treat your chinchilla yourself.

Also, read reviews online of the vet clinic you choose before you go there. All vet clinics are not equal. Reviews will help you eliminate vets who are overly expensive, give poor care, or lack compassion.

Chinchillas do not need annual vaccinations, however, inexperienced owners should schedule a yearly checkup to check their chinchilla's overall health and make sure there's no issues like overgrown teeth.

EARS
The ears should be soft
and velvety with no
rough patches.

FEET
The feet should be
soft and not cracked
and dry. There should
be no scabs or swelling.

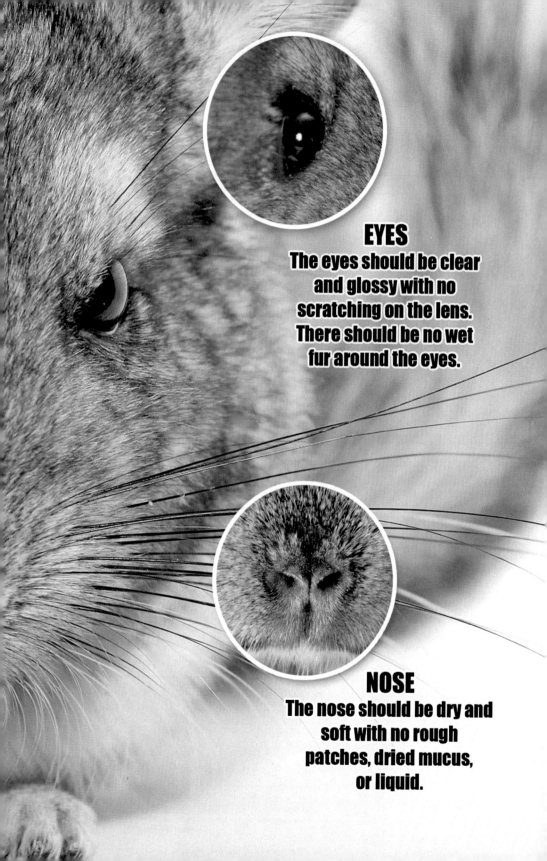

EYES
The eyes should be clear and glossy with no scratching on the lens. There should be no wet fur around the eyes.

NOSE
The nose should be dry and soft with no rough patches, dried mucus, or liquid.

Common Health Issues
Fur Chewing

Fur chewing (barbering) can be caused by environmental factors but it is largely genetic. Fur chewers will chew their own fur constantly until the hair is cut about halfway down. It's very rare that chinchillas will barber down to the skin. Chinchillas will sometimes also chew the fur of their cagemate or offspring. If the fur chewing is hereditary, the chinchilla may chew their fur for their entire life. However, there are a few things you can do to help them chew less frequently.

Chinchillas will chew more when they are stressed out. Keeping your chinchilla in a quiet room where they won't be disturbed can help with the barbering.

Another reason chinchillas will start to fur chew more often is boredom. Give your chinchilla plenty of daily interaction, play time, and socialization. Also, give them plenty of wood chews to distract them.

Once you have eliminated your chinchilla's stress and boredom, the fur chewing may lessen or disappear completely. If the fur chewing continues, don't worry. Fur chewing is not detrimental to the health of your chinchilla.

Ensure you are feeding your chinchilla the proper diet and bathing them in dust specifically made for chinchillas to rule out poor diet and skin irritation as the cause of the fur chewing.

Bloat

Bloat occurs when the intestinal system fills with gas. Chinchillas do not have the ability to burp, so gas can get trapped in the GI system and build up.

Symptoms

A chinchilla with bloat will be less active or lethargic. They may start eating less or stop eating completely. The abdomen will usually feel very firm and be painful to the touch. You may also see a chinchilla with bloat stretching often. The stretching helps relieve the pain. Another symptom to look for is constipation.

Causes

Bloat is often caused by a change in diet. It can also be caused by too many sugary treats, not enough fiber, stress, or overeating.

Treatment

Treatment by a veterinarian immediately may be required to remove the excess gas. Chinchillas can go into stasis and deteriorate quickly, so getting vet care right away is important. After the vet visit, if your chinchilla is not eating you will have to hand feed **Oxbow Critical Care** with a syringe. Critical care is high in fiber and also contains probiotics, vitamins, and minerals that can help clear up the bloat.

Critical Care

You should keep Oxbow Critical Care® on hand at all times. Critical Care® is a wet food meant for hand feeding animals who can't eat their normal diet due to illness, injury, or other ailments. It is high in fiber and contains all essential nutrients needed for proper digestion.

Fungus and Ringworm

Fungal infections such as ringworm are fairly common in chinchillas. Chinchillas' thick fur makes them highly susceptible to ringworm and fungus. Their thick, dense coats absorb humidity which helps provide the perfect growing environment for fungus spores.

Notice the hair loss around the nose and mouth. There is also some scabbing and flaking of the skin.

Symptoms

The first thing you may notice in a chin with a fungal infection is hair loss around the mouth, nose, ears, or eyes. You might also observe red, flakey skin where the hair is missing. The skin can appear crusty, scabby, and dry. Your chinchilla will be itchy and scratching their fur often. If the fungus is ringworm, you may see red circles on the skin.

Treatment

You should take your chinchilla to the vet to get a culture done to determine exactly what type of fungal infection you're dealing with. If your chinchilla is diagnosed with ringworm, Tinactin absorbent powder can be added to your chinchilla's dust bath. Tinactin powder absorbs moisture and cures ringworm and fungal infections. Put one tablespoon of Tinactin with one cup of chinchilla dust in your chinchilla's bath house. If you have more than one chinchilla, use a separate bath house to avoid infecting your other chinchilla. Dust your chinchilla in this mixture for at least 6 weeks. Dust any other chinchillas that have been in contact with the infected chinchilla in this mixture as a preventative measure.

Sanitize the cage and surrounding areas thoroughly. Ringworm spores can cling on dust, dead skin cells, and any surface the infected chinchilla had contact with. Clean all shelves, houses, and cage accessories with an antifungal application.

Ringworm is highly contageous to people and other pets. If your chinchilla is caged with another chinchilla, you will need to move him or her to a separate cage. If you have other pets, move the infected chinchilla into a room with no other animals. Be very careful when handling your chinchilla. Always use gloves.

Causes

Humidity, moisture, moldy hay, and bedding may all lead to fungal infections. It is important to quarantine any new animals for at least 30 days to ensure they do not have any contagious ailments.

It can be passed to chinchillas through infected humans or animals. If someone in your home has athlete's foot, this can cause ringworm in chinchillas. Athlete's foot is is a type of ringworm. If the person with athlete's foot walks on the same surface where your chinchilla roams, they can get infected with the fungus.

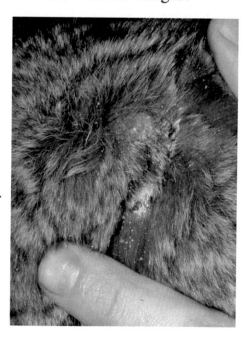

Malocclusion

The term malocclusion literally means "bad bite". In chinchillas, malo is characterized by root or crown elongation either in the molars or incisors. Overgrowth at the crown or surface can cause painful spurs that rub on the inside of the mouth making it painful to eat.

There are three causes of malo. The first is accidental. Chinchillas who fall and break a tooth can develop malo if the tooth grows back abnormally. The second cause of malo is environmental. If chinchillas don't have enough hay or wood to chew on, they will have insufficient tooth wear. Chinchillas have constantly growing molars and incisors. If not worn down, the teeth can grow upwards from the root instead of growing out into the mouth. The roots can grow into the eye socket and the sinuses.

The third cause is genetic. Malo can be passed down from generation to generation. Chinchillas with malo in their genetic background should never be bred.

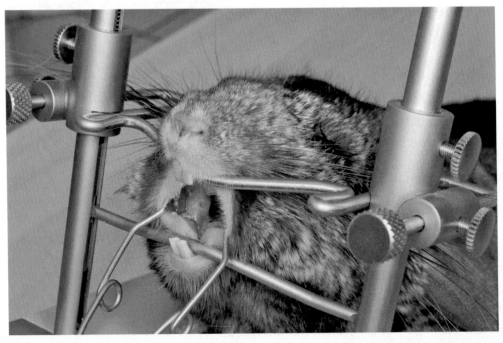

Symptoms

Weight loss	**Pawing at mouth**
Drooling "slobbers"	**Not eating**
Eye tearing	**Small Droppings**

If you notice any of these symptoms, get your chinchilla to a vet immediately. Dental x-rays are extremely important! Early diagnosis and treatment from a veterinarian is the best thing you can do. If you catch malocclusion early, your vet may be able to file or clip down the teeth while your chinchilla is under anesthesia.

After filing or trimming, there is a likelihood of recurrence. Your chinchilla will need regular care to maintain the teeth. Once the teeth in the upper jaw progress upwards toward the eye socket and sinuses, nothing more can be done. In this case, euthanasia is the best option.

This chinchilla is suffering from advanced malocclusion. The wet chin and paws are a huge indication. Chinchillas with malocclusion will drool and wipe their mouth with their paws resulting in their paws also being wet.

Sadly, this chinchilla did not survive. If you notice any of the symptoms of malo, urge your vet to do x-rays right away to determine the best options for treatment.

Respiratory Infections

Upper respiratory infections aren't extremely common in chinchillas, but they do happen every now and then. They are usually caused by poor husbandry and infrequent cage cleaning. The ammonia in the soiled bedding builds up and can irritate the respiratory system.

Chinchillas with a URI will often have wheezy or shallow breathing, sneezing, coughing, teary eys, runny nose, and loss of appetite.

See a vet right away if you notice any of these symptoms. If you do not treat a URI right away, it could progress into something more serious like pneumonia. URIs can be fatal if left untreated.

Veterinarians usually treat respiratory infections with an antibiotic, most commonly Baytril, given orally twice daily. You may also need to hand feed your chinchilla during this time if they are not eating.

Diarrhea and Constipation

If your chinchilla has mushy or squishy stools with no other symptoms, you can try taking away their pellets and only feed timothy hay for 24-48 hours. You can also try feeding them a very small piece of very dark, burnt toast. This will help settle their stomach. If the diarrhea persists for more than 24 hours, your chinchilla will require emergency veterinary care. Prolonged diarrhea can be very serious.

If your chinchilla is not pooping or has very tiny poop, they may be constipated. The first thing you should do is make sure their water bottle is working properly. As with diarrhea, you should eliminate pellets and only feed timothy hay. You can also try feeding Critical Care to get things moving along. It is important to get moisture into their system. If symptoms persist, seek immediate vet care.

Chinchilla Emergency Kit

Listed below are essential items that every chichilla owner should have handy in case of emergencies.

PEDIALYTE	Pedialyte helps replace electrolytes and fluids after diarrhea or overheating.
CRITICAL CARE	Critical Care is used for chinchillas who are not eating.
SYRINGE	Syringes are needed for hand feeding and medicating your chinchilla.
TRAVEL CARRIER	You will need a travel cage or carrier to transport your chinchilla to the vet.
GRAM SCALE	It is important to have a gram scale so you can weigh your chinchilla often to make sure they are not losing weight.
TINACTIN POWDER	Use Tinactin powder in your chinchilla's dust bath to cure or prevent ringworm.
BAG BALM	Bag balm can be applied to dry, cracked feet and ears.
BLU-KOTE	Use Blu-Kote directly on ringworm or fungus. You can also put Blu-Kote directly on wounds to help stop bleeding.
ICE PACK	Always keep an ice pack in your freezer in case your chinchilla overheats.

Accidental Injuries

Even if you do everything correctly, sometimes injuries can still happen. The most common injuries happen as the result of falls.

If you see your chinchilla fall, monitor them very closely. Check your chinchilla's teeth right away to make sure none got broken in the fall. If you see a broken tooth, head to the vet right away. The vet may need to file or trim the teeth to make sure they grow back correctly.

After a fall, you might not notice them acting off at first, but with close examination you may notice that they are lethargic, have a limp, or flinch when touched in certain areas. If you notice any of these signs, take your chinchilla to the vet. They could have broken bones or internal injuries.

If your chinchilla is limping, they may have a broken leg. You need to have a vet treat the leg promptly or the bones can fuse together. Broken legs will

sometimes require amputation. Chinchillas with amputated limbs do very well and most still get around as well as they did before the amputation.

If your chinchilla has an open wound from an accidental fall, fighting with another chinchilla, or any other accident, the treatment will vary depending on the severity of the wound. If you see a small cut or wound, first check for any signs of infection including redness, pus, and inflamation. If you see any sign of infection, take your chinchilla to the vet immediately. If the wound is not infected, apply Neosporin to prevent infection from occurring. If the wound is bleeding, spray Blu-Kote on the wound to stop the bleeding immediately. You can clean the wound with an unscented baby wipe. Monitor daily for signs of infection.

All large cuts or wounds will require prompt veterinary care.

Poisonous Plants

Many household plants can be poisonous to your chinchilla. Listed below are a few common household plants that are toxic. Never allow your chinchilla to have playtime in a room that has any of these plants within reach.

Aloe Vera
Amaryllis
Azalea
Baby's Breath
Begonia
Carnations
Chrysanthemum
Cyclamen
Daffodil
Gladiola

Holly Berries
Hosta
Ivy
Lilies
Morning Glory
Oleander
Poinsettia
Pothos
Tomato Plant
Tulips

Overheating

Chinchillas overheat very easily in any temperatures above 72 degrees fahrenheit. You need to keep your chinchilla in a room that can consistantly stay below that temperature. If you don't have air conditioning, you can purchase a window unit or portable air conditioner.

If you have no way of obtaining an air conditioning unit of any kind and you live in a climate where the temperature regularly reaches over 70 degrees, you should consider rehoming your chinchilla.

If your air conditioner stops working or your home reaches above 72 degrees, there are a few things you can do to keep them cool. Place ice packs around the cage (out of reach of your chinchilla). You can also put a frozen water bottle in your chinchilla's cage. The water bottle needs to be wrapped in fleece to avoid being chewed. Marble or granite slabs can be placed in the freezer and then put in your chinchilla's cage. They will lay on the slab to keep cool. In extreme cases, move your chinchilla into a travel carrier, and place them in front of an open freezer.

The symptoms of overheating are bright red blood vessels in the ears (see below), rapid breathing, red gums and tongue, and lethargy.

If you suspect heatstroke, call your vet immediately for further instructions

CHAPTER 5

Breeding
and More

Breeding

Breeding any animal is a huge responsibility! All new chinchilla owners are strongly discouraged from breeding any of their pet chinchillas. Extensive research needs to be done before even considering starting your own breeding program.

Due to many genetic issues, chinchillas that do not have a pedigree should never be bred.

The careless breeding of non-pedigreed animals has contributed to the increase of malocclusion and fur chewing among pet chinchillas.

The female chinchilla can experience various serious breeding issues during pregnancy. Some of these issues may even be fatal. Breeding should never be taken lightly.

Avoiding Pregnancies

Accidental pregnancies are easy to avoid if you follow these steps:

*Properly sex your chinchillas
*Do not allow opposite sexes to play together
*Keep cages far enough away
*Do not house members of the opposite sex together
*Neutering

How to Sex Your Chinchilla

Properly sexing all of your chinchillas will help prevent any unwanted pregnancies. Pet stores and uneducated breeders mis-sex chinchillas often. Always double check the sex of your chinchilla to make sure no mistakes were made. They can be difficult to sex, so it's important to know what to look for.

FEMALE

In females, the cone and anus are very close together. There will also be a slit in the cone.

MALE

In males, the cone and anus are much farther apart. The cone will have no slit, and with slight pressure, the penis will protrude.

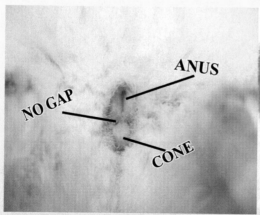

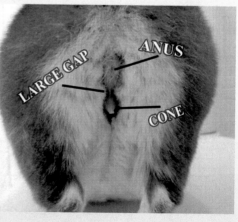

You should never allow chinchillas of the opposite sex to play together. You might think that a few seconds together is not a big deal, and you could break them up before they mate. In reality, it only takes seconds for them to mate.

You will also need to place their cages a safe distance apart. Chinchillas can mate through the bars of the cage if they're too close.

Pregnancy

Chinchillas reach sexual maturity at around 7-8 months of age, but some have been known to get pregnant as young as four months old. They are pregnant for approximately 111 days. Males and females will breed even if they are related.

It is nearly impossible to tell if a chinchilla is pregnant or not until it's close to the delivery date. The easiest way to tell is by feeling the nipples. If your chinchilla has long, thin nipples, she could be pregnant.

If your chinchilla is pregnant, there are a few different things you will need to do. First, switch from timothy to alfalfa hay since it has more calcium and protein.

If you have the male and female together in the same cage, remove the male to avoid back breeding. Chinchillas can get pregnant soon after delivery, and it's very hard on them to be pregnant back to back.

Keep the female in a calm, stress free environment. Make sure she is in a quiet, low traffic area of the house. Too much stress could cause her to abort the fetuses. Try not to handle her too often while she is pregnant, and monitor her closely for any sign of distress.

If you suspect that something is wrong at any point, call your vet immediately.

Birth and Kits

Baby chinchillas are called "kits" (or "kittens"). They are born fully covered in fur with their eyes open. They are able to completely walk around shortly after birth. The average litter size is 1-3 kits.

Most chinchillas can deliver successfully on their own with no human intervention. Observe the birth, and don't step in unless you notice any birthing complications. If the female has been in labor for 3-4 hours with no delivery, looks restless, has lost a lot of blood, or is very vocal, call an experienced vet immediately.

You will need to have a gram scale ready so you can weigh the kits daily to make sure they are gaining weight. Monitor them carefully to ensure they are nursing. To help your female produce more milk, you can add a second water bottle with half cranberry or apple juice (no sugar added) and half water.

Kits need to be in a cage with bar spacing 1/4 inch or less or they can escape. You will also want to remove any high ledges to avoid the mother accidentally jumping down and injuring them. Remove any wheel you may have.

Handle the kits daily. The more you socialize with them, the friendlier they will be. Kits are usually weaned at around 8 weeks old, but they should stay with the mother until they are at least 12 weeks. Separate any male kits from the mother and any female siblings after 12 weeks to avoid future pregnancies.

Male chinchillas can be neutered if you need to keep a male and female pair together. The male can still get the female pregnant up to 6 weeks after the neuter. They will need to be separated during this time.

CHAPTER 6

Everything Else

Chinchillas With Other Pets

If you have other pets in your house, you may be wondering if you can let your chinchilla interact with them. Some pets you can never let around your chinchilla. Others can be allowed in the same room with proper supervision. However, chinchillas should never be housed in the same cage with any other species.

CATS	Cats can carry the Bordetella and Pasteurella bacteria which are contageous to chinchillas. Cats may also see your chinchilla as prey. Scratches and bites can happen in the blink of an eye. Cats have even been known to attack chinchillas through the cage bars. Take extreme caution when having chinchillas and cats in the same house.
DOGS	If your dog has a strong prey drive, never allow them around your chinchilla. Even gentle dogs can accidentally injure your chinchilla by jumping on them or playing too rough. Always supervise your dog around your chinchilla.
RABBITS	Over half of all rabbits carry the Pasteurella bacteria. Most never show symptoms, but they are still able to transmit the bacteria to other animals. Chinchillas can easily catch Pasteurella and get extremely ill. Never allow rabbits and chinchillas to play together, and keep them caged in separate rooms.
GUINEA PIGS	Guinea pigs and chinchillas can be caged in the same room. If you do allow them to play together, monitor them very closely. Your chinchilla could accidentally jump and land on your guinea pig causing injury.
RATS	Rats and chinchillas should be caged far away from each other. Rats have very sensitive respiratory systems and the dust from your chinchilla's dust bath can make them sick.

Purchasing Your Chinchilla

Check your local humane society and shelters for chinchillas in need of a good home. Thousands of chinchillas a year are surrendered by families who can no longer care for them.

If you can't find a chinchilla at your local shelter, look for a responsible breeder. Check reviews online and make sure the breeder you purchase from is reputable.

Avoid purchasing your chinchilla from a pet store. These animals often come from large breeding mills where they are kept in filthy, crowded conditions. When you purchase an animal from one of these stores, it helps contribute to these terrible practices. You also won't know the genetic background of the chinchilla you're purchasing.

If you already own a chinchilla, you need to quarantine any new chinchillas for at least 30 days before introducing them.

Introductions

When you get a new chinchilla, you need to introduce them together slowly and carefully. Keep in mind that not all chinchillas will get along no matter how hard you try.

After the 30 day quarantine period, you can allow them to have supervised playtime in a neutral area for short periods of time. You can also place their cages a few feet from each other to get them used to each other's scent. Once playtime goes well for a few weeks, you can try caging them together. Remove any items that either chinchilla could be territorial over. Wash all items to remove any scent Make the cage as neutral as possible so one chinchilla doesn't feel like it's his or her territory.

Owner Stories & Experiences

"My little guy Bruce was a birthday present for me from my boyfriend. I had always wanted a chinchilla, and I was so excited! He instantly grew a bond with me and would sit on my shoulder when I walked around the house. Whenever we walk into the bedroom, if we do not say hi to him within the first couple of minutes, he will squeak at us until we do. Such amazing animals!"
-Cassandra Littell

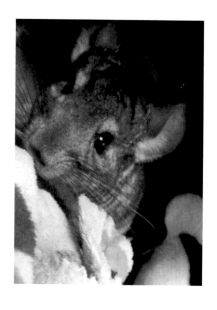

"I would like to tell how loveable my chin is. No, he wont sit in my lap while I watch a movie. However, I get exhausted very fast from a medical condition. When I am having a 'bad day', he just watches me like a little nurse. When I take him to his playroom, he stops in the middle of what he is doing to come check on me. Once I tell him I'm ok, he will scamper off again. They have their own ways of showing how much they care for their 'fur parents'."
-Cathy Hardesty

"We love being chin parents, but it hasn't always been great or easy. I got an 8 week old mosiac chin for Christmas in 2012 from my husband. We unfortunately lost him in Feburary of 2014. Scout was fun, adorable, and a handful - complete opposite of our lazy, relaxed chinchilla Diego! One morning, my husband woke up to a loud ruckus from the chin room and ran out, but by that time it was already too late. Scout had stuck his head into a hanging hay ball that he had in his cage since we got him with no problems. In a matter of seconds of struggling, he broke his neck and was gone. We were devastated, and it was one of the hardest days of my life. Be very careful as many things labeled for chinchillas are not safe, and be very wary of any items with gaps that a chinchilla could possibly stick their arm or legs into and get stuck. If you question it, do not use it. We wouldn't want anyone to go through what we did with our Baby Scout."

-Shelby Marie Williams

"Before I got my chinnies, I did all my research. Looked into cages, bedding, diet, toys etc. I thought I was pretty well prepared...... until I got them. Then POOP! Poop everywhere! I was not prepared for the amount of poop that these little guys leave everywhere! After playtime, I find little 'presents' behind the sofa, on the tv, and in my drink! To anyone buying a chinchilla, buy a handheld Hoover! Its a Godsend!"
-Shaney Leigh

"Mylo was hand fed as a kit, and we became incredibly close. He now sleeps in my bed and wears hats I make him. He doesn't like to travel or be combed, but he loves modeling hats."
-Mel Badger Smith

"I never intended on owning a chinchilla. I worked for an animal shelter when I acquired Gigi. I received a phone call one day from my local animal control saying that they had "some type of small animal" and didn't know what it was. I went to pick up the two small animals (one being a guinea pig) and saw that the second one was a chinchilla. They were abandoned in an apartment for some time and then abandoned overnight outside the shelter by the landlord with a note. I brought both animals home for the night with the intent to bring them both to work the next morning. I had always been fascinated with chinchillas and took a liking to her immediately. She was in rough shape, not eating, not going to the bathroom and very thin. Her coat was greasy and disheveled. She had been offered poor quality guinea pig food and had no exercise wheel, hammock or hay. I went out and bought her each of these items. I brought the guinea pig to work and decided to keep the chinchilla as a foster to get her in better health. She was in a small starter cage and had minimal accessories. I went out and bought her Oxbow chinchilla food and high quality hay. First, I had to syringe feed her critical care and administer subcutaneous fluids for almost a week before she started to perk up and eat and drink on her own. I had to bring her back and forth to work with me daily. During this time we really started to bond, and I started getting attached to Gigi. I soon brought home a very large ferret cage for her and decorated it with all sorts of hammocks and fleece items. She soon had everything she needed and was doing very well and eating on her own. After several dust baths her coat really improved and looked normal and healthy. After putting so much care and time into her I really bonded with her and could not bring her back to the shelter. I finalized her adoption and have spoiled her rotten ever since. She has been an absolute joy to have and has brought me so much happiness every day. She is very social and sweet. She will always have a permanent home with me."

-Danielle Wilson

"I have owned chinchillas since I was 8, and I went 11 years without needing a vet for emergencies. I had a vet number, but rarely visited the clinic. I left my home for one night, and left my pets in the care of my mother. There was an accident, and when I came home my mom told me that somehow an unfamiliar cat got into the chinchilla room. He had torn her chest open from her upper shoulder, down past her arm pit. It was late, and it was Saturday night. I immediately cleaned her up and tried calling the vet number I had but the clinic had shut down. I stayed up until 3 am calling all vet practices (farm, domestic, wildlife centers). I had to leave voicemails for some, and I was a mess. First thing the next morning. I received a call back from ONE vet's office, 45 minutes away willing to take us the moment we arrived. They took care of Aurora on a Sunday morning. She had to have surgery and had to go back for re-stitching and cleanings multiple times. She was also pregnant at this time, so this vet was very careful with her. We were lucky, and blessed to get that one call back out of so many. Now, Aurora is alive and well. Her kit also survived, and Aurora delivered him on her own and even nursed him while she continued her treatment and therapy. I tell everyone to find a vet, and make sure it is all current information. Dr. Lee is our vet for all cases, and we visit her many times a year. We take our pet chins and rescue chins to her with any and all concerns we have. We're blessed to have a clinic near us that is open 7 days a week from 6am to 9-10pm."

-Amber Gold

"It was my brown velvet chinchilla, Cream's, first litter. She had given birth to a little baby girl. While busy birthing her son, she was confused as to what to do and ignored the still wet baby. So I took her and pressed her to my bosom, wrapping her with me in my bathrobe. She dried quickly and was fine. Once Cream was done with her boy, I put her back with mom. Cream was unfortunately not making much milk so I bottle fed the little girl, later named Sugar. I felt so close to that little one, bottle feeding her and even having her nap in my sleeves, against my bosom or just against me. I truly felt like the most important person in this little girl's life and it was easy to see that she depended me. It had to be the best experience I had with a chinchilla and it will be forever remembered."

-Stephanie Demers

"My boyfriend and I were looking for a small pet. I originally wanted a kitten, but my landlord wouldn't allow cats. We looked into chinchillas and fell in love! I went looking on Craigslist for a chinchilla and came across a one year old chinchilla named Mrs. Puff. I just knew she was perfect for us! We brought her home and I immediately started spoiling her! About a month later, we got quite a surprise! I heard squeaks coming from her cage. I couldn't see anything because she was in her house. I lifted the house and found Chichi tending to dark black female kit! I was shocked! I had no clue she was pregnant! Chichi later had a mosaic male kit, too! We named the male Tribble and the female Tia. I ended up getting three chinchillas for the price of one! We love our little chinchilla family. It has been quite a trip watching the babies grow up. Chichi is now 5 years old and the babies will be 4 in October! They bring us so much joy each and every day!"

- Kay Molnar

"My ex and I were living in a 1 bedroom apartment with the chinchillas. The chin cage was located in the living room and the chins were allowed an hour of out of the cage time every night. After a night of playtime, my ex noticed that her car keys were missing. She scolded me because she was sure that it was me playing a trick on her. Three days later, we were cleaning out the chin cages, and guess what we found inside of their hidey house: her car keys. The chins stole them and hid them from us in their cage. My ex used to joke that it was their way of saying 'don't ever leave us'."
-Doug Bouffard

"I don't own my chinchillas, all 3 definitely own me. Loved them since I was a kid, and a family friend showed me how they bathe and wall surf and finally had the chance to adopt one I found posted online - I've obtained another 2 since, and if I had the room I'd own more! They aren't the best pets for everyone - but they are perfect for our family"
-Jennifer Winn

"I've always been amazed at how, for lack of a better word, intuitive CrashIntoMe has been about my moods. Shortly after I first adopted him from a chin rescue in Ohio, I had a fight with my now ex, and to calm myself, I started cleaning the chinchilla cage. I got as far as sitting on the floor beside it with the door open before the crying fit took hold, and I stayed there for a good five minutes just getting it out of my system. During that five minutes, Crash used his contact call multiple times and eventually climbed over to me on the shelf nearest the door. After a minute of sniffing me over, he found my face and put his paw on my nose to sniff me better. I froze, nervous to let him that close to my eyes, but that was a mistake. To help me feel better, he cuddled up against my cheek and gently groomed my eyebrow with his teeth, shaving about a 1/4" patch of hair completely bald. Then he realized my nose was far more interesting and tried to stick his paw in my nostril to see if it needed groomed too, by which point I was laughing so hard the tears started again. He really is a sweet, caring little ball of fur that seems as in tune with our emotions as any dog or cat would be, and I'm so blessed to have my chins in my life. "

- Rebecca Hahn

I'd like to thank my chinchillas **Yuki** and **Momo** for always being there for me. Without them, this book would not be possible.

Table of Contents

Table of Contents

Thanks for reading
Pet Chinchillas the
Complete Care Guide!

Made in the USA
San Bernardino, CA
08 December 2015